PISCES

HOROSCOPE

& ASTROLOGY

2023

Mystic Cat

Suite 41906, 3/2237 Gold Coast HWY

Mermaid Beach, Queensland, 4218

Australia

Contents

PISCES 2023
HOROSCOPE & ASTROLOGY

Four Weeks Per Month

Week 1 – Days 1 - 7

Week 2 – Days 8 - 14

Week 3 – Days 15 - 21

Week 4 – Days 22 – Month-end

PISCES

Pisces Dates: February 19th to March 20th
Zodiac Symbol: Pair of Fish
Element: Water
Planets: Jupiter, Neptune
House: Twelfth
Colors: Purple, white

2023 AT A GLANCE

Eclipses

Hybrid Solar – April 20th

Penumbral Lunar – May 5th

Annular Solar – October 14th

Partial Lunar -October 28th

Equinoxes and Solstices

Spring - March 20th 21:25

Summer - June 21st 14:52

Fall – September 23rd 06:50

Winter – December 22nd 03:28

Mercury Retrogrades

December 29th Capricorn - January 18th Capricorn

April 21st Taurus – May 15th Taurus

August 23rd Virgo – September 15th Virgo

December 13th Capricorn - January 2nd, Sagittarius

2023 FULL MOONS

Wolf Moon: January 6th 23:09

Snow Moon: February 13th, 18:30

Worm Moon March 7th, 12:40

Pink Moon: April 6th, 04:37

Flower Moon: May 5th, 17:34

Strawberry Moon: June 4th, 03:42

Buck Moon: July 3rd, 11:40

Sturgeon Moon: August 1st, 18:32

Blue Moon: August 31st, 01:36

Corn, Harvest Moon: September 29th, 06:50

Hunters Moon: October 28th, 20:23

Beaver Moon: November 27th, 09:16

Cold Moon: December 27th, 00:34

2023 INGRESSES

When a planet moves into a new sign or house of the zodiac, it ingresses into the next area. This planetary movement creates an energy shift that can affect your life on many levels. It changes the tone, flavor, and energetic expression of life. Changing cosmic alignments can have detrimental or beneficial impacts on your life.

Some celestial bodies change every few days, others every few weeks, a few only have changes occurring every few years. The longer the time interval between a planet's ingress, the slower the effect on your life.

Cosmic vibrations ripple around your energy field and help raise your vibration, or conversely, lower your energy. It brings a time of change that can affect your life on many levels. Being aware of upcoming changes helps you research and stay mindful of how planetary ingresses may affect your world.

Faster Moving Ingresses

Mar 25, 2023, 11:46	Mars enters Cancer
May 20, 2023, 15:32	Mars enters Leo
Jul 10, 2023, 11:41	Mars enters Virgo
Aug 27, 2023, 13:20	Mars enters Libra
Oct 12, 2023, 04:04	Mars enters Scorpio
Nov 24, 2023, 10:15	Mars enters Sagittarius

Faster Moving Ingresses

Jan 3, 2023, 02:10	Venus enters Aquarius
Jan 27, 2023, 02:33	Venus enters Pisces
Feb 20, 2023, 07:56	Venus enters Aries
Mar 16, 2023, 22:34	Venus enters Taurus
Apr 11, 2023, 04:48	Venus enters Gemini
May 7, 2023, 14:25	Venus enters Cancer
Jun 5, 2023, 13:47	Venus enters Leo
Oct 9, 2023, 01:11	Venus enters Virgo
Nov 8, 2023, 09:31	Venus enters Libra
Dec 4, 2023, 18:51	Venus enters Scorpio
Dec 29, 2023, 20:24	Venus enters Sagittarius
Feb 11, 2023, 11:23	Mercury enters Aquarius
Mar 2, 2023, 22:52	Mercury enters Pisces
Mar 19, 2023, 04:24	Mercury enters Aries
Apr 3, 2023, 16:22	Mercury enters Taurus
Jun 11, 2023, 10:27	Mercury enters Gemini
Jun 27, 2023, 00:24	Mercury enters Cancer
Jul 11, 2023, 04:11	Mercury enters Leo

Faster Moving Ingresses

Jul 28, 2023, 21:32   Mercury enters Virgo

Oct 5, 2023, 00:09   Mercury enters Libra

Oct 22, 2023, 06:49   Mercury enters Scorpio

Nov 10, 2023, 06:25   Mercury enters Sagittarius

Dec 1, 2023, 14:32   Mercury enters Capricorn

Slower Moving Ingresses

Mar 7, 2023, 13:35   Saturn enters Pisces

Mar 23, 2023, 12:14   Pluto enters Aquarius

May 16, 2023, 17:21   Jupiter enters Taurus

THE MOON PHASES

- New Moon (Dark Moon)

- Waxing Crescent Moon

- First Quarter Moon

- Waxing Gibbous Moon

- Full Moon

- Waning Gibbous (Disseminating) Moon

- Third (Last/Reconciling) Quarter Moon

- Waning Crescent (Balsamic) Moon

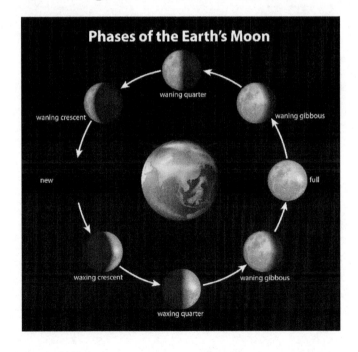

2023

JANUARY
M	T	W	T	F	S	S
						1
2	3	4	5	6	7	8
9	10	11	12	13	14	15
16	17	18	19	20	21	22
23	24	25	26	27	28	29
30	31					

FEBRUARY
M	T	W	T	F	S	S
		1	2	3	4	5
6	7	8	9	10	11	12
13	14	15	16	17	18	19
20	21	22	23	24	25	26
27	28					

MARCH
M	T	W	T	F	S	S
		1	2	3	4	5
6	7	8	9	10	11	12
13	14	15	16	17	18	19
20	21	22	23	24	25	26
27	28	29	30	31		

APRIL
M	T	W	T	F	S	S
					1	2
3	4	5	6	7	8	9
10	11	12	13	14	15	16
17	18	19	20	21	22	23
24	25	26	27	28	29	30

MAY
M	T	W	T	F	S	S
1	2	3	4	5	6	7
8	9	10	11	12	13	14
15	16	17	18	19	20	21
22	23	24	25	26	27	28
29	30	31				

JUNE
M	T	W	T	F	S	S
			1	2	3	4
5	6	7	8	9	10	11
12	13	14	15	16	17	18
19	20	21	22	23	24	25
26	27	28	29	30		

JULY
M	T	W	T	F	S	S
					1	2
3	4	5	6	7	8	9
10	11	12	13	14	15	16
17	18	19	20	21	22	23
24	25	26	27	28	29	30
31						

AUGUST
M	T	W	T	F	S	S
1	2	3	4	5	6	
7	8	9	10	11	12	13
14	15	16	17	18	19	20
21	22	23	24	25	26	27
28	29	30	31			

SEPTEMBER
M	T	W	T	F	S	S
				1	2	3
4	5	6	7	8	9	10
11	12	13	14	15	16	17
18	19	20	21	22	23	24
25	26	27	28	29	30	

OCTOBER
M	T	W	T	F	S	S
						1
2	3	4	5	6	7	8
9	10	11	12	13	14	15
16	17	18	19	20	21	22
23	24	25	26	27	28	29
30	31					

NOVEMBER
M	T	W	T	F	S	S
		1	2	3	4	5
6	7	8	9	10	11	12
13	14	15	16	17	18	19
20	21	22	23	24	25	26
27	28	29	30			

DECEMBER
M	T	W	T	F	S	S
				1	2	3
4	5	6	7	8	9	10
11	12	13	14	15	16	17
18	19	20	21	22	23	24
25	26	27	28	29	30	31

Time set to Coordinated Universal Time Zone

(UT±0)

Meteor Showers are on the date they peak.

Sun	Mon	Tue	Wed	Thu	Fri	Sat
1	2	3	4	5	6	7
8	9	10	11	12	13	14
15	16	17	18	19	20	21
22	23	24	25	26	27	28
29	30	31				

January 3rd - Quadrantids Meteor Shower. Jan 1st-5th

January 6th - Wolf Moon. Full Moon in Cancer 23:09

January 7th - Mercury at Inferior Conjunction

January 12th - Mars Retrograde ends in Gemini

January 15th - Last Quarter Moon in Libra 02:10

January 18th - Mercury Retrograde ends in Capricorn

January 21st - New Moon in Aquarius 20:55

January 22nd - Uranus Retrograde ends in Taurus January 22nd - Chinese New Year (Rabbit)

January 28th - First Quarter Moon in Taurus 15:19

January 30th - Mercury at Greatest Elong: 25.0°W

FULL MOON

JANUARY WEEK ONE

The Quadrantids Meteor Shower blazes across the night sky this week. A full Moon in Cancer draws insight. Looking at your goals deeper provides you with valuable insight. If you find that your life is lacking, you need to do more to improve the prospects in your world. It brings a time to let go of the past and move on towards brighter prospects for your life. Engaging in meditation and introspection helps release the past. Removing attachments opens a new chapter in your life. Carrying past lessons into the next stage of your life enables you to set the bar higher. You soon head towards a new possibility that offers to nurture stability and well-being in your life.

Moving in alignment with your emotions, dreams, and aspirations lets you chart a course to develop your life. You discover new options ahead, spark growth and bring abundance into your life. Your intuition helps guide a journey that offers peace, stability, and balanced growth in your personal life. Allowing yourself to merge your dreams with someone who inspires your life enables you to reach a goal that transforms your situation. It draws excellent meaning and purpose into your life. It brings growth to your love life. Positive momentum enables you to develop shared goals and dreams that nurture romance and magic in your life. Trusting your instincts allow you to offer your hopes and dreams to another person who lights up your life in many ways.

Mars retrograde ends in Gemini. Doing due diligence, being resourceful, and working towards your plan grow your career path. Advancement is in the pipeline; a new role emerges in your life that brings a new level of expertise and experience into your working life. Preparation and planning gather your resources as you set to work and plot a course towards success. Implementing plans and developing your career path hold you in good stead. By studying and refining your abilities, you realize you have the skills and capabilities required to achieve a successful result. You create progress and achieve significant goals by creating a comprehensive blueprint to take you towards the success you seek. Study and educational pursuits lead to a blossoming path forward for your career goals.

A sudden understanding clears the path ahead and provides you with insight and encouragement as you embark on nurturing new ideas. You thrive on highly original and creative thinking, inspiration, and motivation which helps you pursue intellectual and creative opportunities that cross your path. Improving your circumstances be challenging but rewarding. Exploring higher education and learning pursuits help you channel your energy effectively to enhance your life. Keeping your mindset optimistic enables you to deal with hurdles and challenges along the way. You discover it is worthwhile to grow your world as you champion a cause close to your heart.

Mercury retrograde ends in Capricorn. A New Moon in Aquarius at the week's end brings fresh energy. You enter a productive and active phase that gives you security and stability as you work towards your vision for future growth. Assessing and refining your plans establish a sound development clip through careful planning and preparation. You find options to learn and refine your skills ahead. Your determination helps you turn a corner and expand your possibilities outwardly. Your commitment to improving your circumstances attracts an abundant landscape. A new role emerges for your career path. This exciting option tempts you to advance your skills and develop your talents. Moving in alignment with your inspiration provides you with security, happiness, and stability. Your commitment to excel bring a rewarding result into your life.

It brings skill development, financial opportunity, and progress into your life. Setting aspirations and planning for future growth help you blend your goals with the essence of manifestation to advance your career path forward. The outlook looks promising and upcoming changes signify you enjoy rising prospects in your working life. Examining the way ahead enables you to reach for gold and achieve growth that brings abundance and stability into your life. It offers a new beginning that drives inspiration and motivates you to work towards your goals. A windfall is possible as you refine your abilities and learn how to turn your dreams into reality.

Chinese New Year of the Rabbit. Creative expression figures prominently in your life as you experience all that life has to offer. Discovering different approaches to expressing yourself brings an expansive and fulfilling journey forward for your life. Reflecting on the possibilities surrounding your life, ground your energy and open up an abundant landscape that nurtures stability, joy, and happiness. It points you towards a path of creativity, growth, and change. A fruitful and loving harvest of promise is showing up in your life soon.

Change and discovery ahead remind you that the wheel is always turning in your life, taking you towards new options. Good luck and rising prospects make themselves known and enable you to advance your studies forward. And advancement comes into your career path. Setting intentions and visualizing reinforces your goals as you grow and expand life outwardly. Excitement, happiness, and inspiration flow freely into your world. Your dreams shine brightly, and you feel peaceful and centered as you begin growing the path ahead. Karmic forces are at the crux of your choices and decisions regarding your future career path. Keeping life balanced, you reconnect with the passion within your heart. Setting intentions for this Chinese year brings a cycle of good fortune and prosperity into your life.

FEBRUARY

Sun	Mon	Tue	Wed	Thu	Fri	Sat
			1	2	3	4
5	6	7	8	9	10	11
12	13	14	15	16	17	18
19	20	21	22	23	24	25
26	27	28				

February 1st - Imbolc

February 5th - Snow Moon. Full Moon in Leo 18:30

February 13th - Last Quarter Moon in Scorpio 16:01

February 16th - Saturn in Conjunction with Sun

February 20th - New Moon in Pisces 07:08

February 27th - First Quarter Moon in Gemini 08:06

NEW MOON

FULL MOON

A Full Moon in Leo brings some challenges, and you focus on the past with sadness and regret. Old wounds and bitter memories flood your mind and delay progress in your life. Releasing the past; healing your spirit helps you move towards greener pastures and reflect on the valuable lessons learned to hold you in good stead. New opportunities and possibilities are waiting in the wings for you when you are ready to open your life up to a new interest. Looking on the bright side helps release outworn energy and sadness during this Full Moon. If you feel caught up with sentimental and melancholy thoughts, creating space to nurture your surroundings draws well-being and balance into your world.

Soul-searching and contemplation bring stability that helps you navigate life's challenges and steer towards smoother water. Approaching life calmly, you remain steady and upbeat even when faced with issues or drama in your social life. You make intelligent decisions and grow your world balanced and sustainable. New possibilities enter your social life. Being open to new people and possibilities brings unique friendships into your life. Extending your life in a new direction brings peace and stability into your world. You begin to attract the correct type of people into your world as you know how to move away from negativity and head towards a path that nurtures peace, harmony, love, and happiness.

Love blossoms and thrives with the care and attention you bestow on your personal life. You discover that you are on the same wavelength and have shared goals with someone you care deeply about in your life. You share a blissful and expansive chapter with someone who inspires you a great deal with thoughtful gestures and an attentive and loving approach. Life ahead brings moments to cherish as you get busy bonding and developing your romantic life.

This week gives you insight into your deeper feelings and emotional awareness surrounding your love life. It brings an emotionally rewarding time of growing your love life in a warm and loving direction. Investing your time and energy in your personal life gets tangible results. Sharing tender moments with someone who lights up your life offers heightened stability and emotional well-being. Feelings of love and happiness abound, and this gives you the signal to grow your life and begin sharing more profound thoughts with someone who inspires your life on many levels.

Singles discover that a social aspect ahead encourages rising prospects in your personal life. It brings new dreams to light that offers true happiness and abundance. You forge a bond with a kindred spirit and nurture this situation gently, progressively, and sustainably. Seeing the big picture of what is possible in your love life gives you insight and clarity into the path ahead.

Saturn is in conjunction with the Sun. A New Moon in Pisces signifies that something important will appear in your life soon. It attracts an enriching time that lines you up with unique possibilities. Positive change ahead brings goodness to the top as you unearth new opportunities for your life. It places you in the box seat to form new friends as it widens your social circle. An invitation ahead lets you treat yourself to a relaxing and happy time shared with friends. Connecting with people you hold near and dear over the coming weeks draws rejuvenation and abundance into your life. An opportunity hits a sweet note in your social life. Your confidence rises and attracts the correct type of people into your life. Having an abundant social life draws stability and nurtures magic in your world. It brings stimulating discussions that link you with an enriching time of sharing thoughts with someone compatible with your life.

Life settles into a more manageable groove that links you up with security, stability, and progress. It transitions you towards a journey of great promise that strengthens your life by improving your circumstances. It has you feel more energized and ready to tackle new projects as you launch your skills towards growing your world. It brings the right platform from which to express new dreams and goals.

Two minds are better than one; you find that joining forces with a co-conspirator raises the potential possible in your life. It brings a time of sharing thoughts and ideas with someone who inspires you greatly. Opening a dialogue with someone you trust gets the ball rolling on developing shared goals and aspirations that help launch your ship of dreams.

A busy time ahead see you juggling your roles, responsibilities, and priorities. Finding balance within a dynamic and active environment be your ticket to success. Happiness and harmony result from the care and attention to detail you get to the tasks at hand. It heads you towards maintaining a balanced home/working life. Establishing a stable routine helps you gain traction on a successful career path. It brings a breakthrough moment that advances your life towards new prospects.

You discover an opportunity that lets you claim your authority as a leader. It brings a new role that advances life towards a lofty goal. Masterfully applying your talents enables you to climb the ladder towards success in your working life. A systematic, organized, and strategic approach Bring fruitful results into your life. Leaning into your strengths places you in the proper alignment to achieve growth in your career path. You discover a career option that feels like the right choice for your life.

MARCH

Sun	Mon	Tue	Wed	Thu	Fri	Sat
			1	2	3	4
5	6	7	8	9	10	11
12	13	14	15	16	17	18
19	20	21	22	23	24	25
26	27	28	29	30	31	

March 7th - Worm Moon. Full Moon in Virgo 12:40

March 15th - Last Quarter Moon: Sagittarius 02:08
March 15th - Neptune in Conjunction with Sun

March 17th - Mercury at Superior Conjunction

March 20th - Ostara/Spring Equinox 21:25

March 21st - New Moon in Pisces 17:22

March 29th - First Quarter Moon in Cancer 02:32

FULL MOON

A Full Moon in Virgo brings a clear pool of understanding that reflects inner awareness. Weighing up your options helps you avoid staying stuck and being at an impasse. Everything is not as straightforward as it seems; you need to trust your intuition and be guided by your gut instincts as you make a choice ahead for your life. You head to a crossroads in your life and feel a little overwhelmed and unsure about where to head next. Engaging in inner reflection, stepping back from your usual routine, and listening to your intuition bring you the wisdom that grows the path ahead. A new option crops up for your career path; it involves choices and decisions that feel uncomfortable but ultimately lead to growth and evolution.

You see your life through a more transparent lens as things begin to take shape in your life path. New energy spurs creative visions and grows ideas that connect you with a more profound life purpose. As a master of your destiny, you discover that you make choices and decisions that elevate the potential possible in your world. It brings a more active social life that grows your confidence as you broaden your circle of friends. Take a bold move forward and see you move forward with purpose towards your vision. You accomplish a great deal by being open to new people and experiences. Your life expands outwardly, bringing growth and advancement. A unique person enters your life and offers a fresh start that feels inspiring on many levels.

With Mercury getting settled in your first house of privacy, refuge, and seclusion, it brings an appropriate time to look deeper at the people that surround your life. Soul-searching and introspection help you gain insight into personal matters.

The planet Mercury in your first house points you towards a path that draws personal growth to the forefront of your life. Indeed, overcoming problems that be a thorn in your side develops your life in a unique direction. It brings a time of personal growth that cuts through illusions. It enables you to see a broader review of your situation. Various options get the right path through this time. Challenged on many levels, you find the answers needed to grow your life in a new direction. It brings insight and revelations to dispel doubt and help you find the correct path forward for your life.

You may find that someone tries to gain an advantage over your good nature; you need to keep your eyes open and alert. Being on the lookout for sneaky behavior and disingenuous types help you spot the impostor within your social ranks. You find that listening to your intuition enables you to spot issues early on. When something does not feel right or seems fake on some level, trusting your instincts helps you pivot away from problems. Taking things slowly with new friends and companions helps build trust over time and draws balance into your world.

The Spring Equinox this week is an exciting time as someone comes into your life with energy, passion, and enthusiasm. Fuelled by a desire to get to know you better, this person be bold and forthright. You find yourself feeling ready for a new adventure in your social life. Growth and expansion accompany you in expanding your life. Pursuing your goals with confidence drives your enthusiasm and brings you the courage to push back the barriers and head for your dreams. Your life heats up with new energy; life comes to meet you with new possibilities and avenues of growth. A co-conspirator have you dreaming big about the possibilities as things heat up in terms of potential.

New inspiration brings a bevy of opportunities into your life that offers room to redefine the potential possible in your world. It gets a new direction that kicks limitations to the curb as it provides growth and forwards momentum. An exciting, unique opportunity gives you a boost and advancement in your career. Ideas and inspiration be flowing freely, motivating, inspiring, and encouraging you to pursue a new path. Things heat up in your social life, as new prospects have you feeling excited and enthusiastic about developing interpersonal bonds. It is a fertile landscape that enables you to extend your reach and grow your dreams. You attract new possibilities that put you on a fulfilling and enriching journey ahead.

Mars sets up camp in your ninth house of purpose this week. It brings a time that sparks interest in a course or other higher education opportunity. Your inspiration is fuelled by learning a new area and gaining wisdom and mastery over your career path. It brings an active and dynamic time that advances your skills. Being proactive and exploring leads lets you take control of the reins as you move towards achieving your career growth. Establishing yourself in new career potential brings a sweet note into your life. It helps you chart a course towards success and advancement in your working life.

New goals and an inspiring vision help raise confidence. Implementing functional changes grows your life in a structured and balanced manner. You can reshuffle the deck and come out with advancement for your career path. It's a time imbued with possibility and potential. It offers to refine and upskill your talents into a new area.

You are on a beautiful journey towards improving your circumstances. You soon ground your energy in an area that lets you gain traction on developing an exciting goal. Opportunity comes knocking and brings expansion into your life. Experimenting and exploring options brings the right flavor into your life. It positions you to achieve growth and progress life forward onto new endeavors. You soon receive news about an offer that feels tempting and tailor-made for your life.

APRIL

Sun	Mon	Tue	Wed	Thu	Fri	Sat
						1
2	3	4	5	6	7	8
9	10	11	12	13	14	15
16	17	18	19	20	21	22
23	24	25	26	27	28	29
30						

April 6th - Pink Moon. Full Moon in Libra 04:37

April 11th - Jupiter in Conjunction with Sun
April 11th - Mercury at Greatest Elong: 19.5°E

April 13th - Last Quarter Moon in Capricorn 09:11

April 20th - New Moon in Taurus 04:12
April 20th - Hybrid Solar Eclipse

April 21st - Mercury Retrograde begins in Taurus

April 22nd - Lyrids Meteor Shower. April 16-25

April 27th - First Quarter Moon in Leo 21:20

NEW MOON

FULL MOON

The Full Moon in Libra draws insight and introspection into your world. Thinking about things on a deeper level brings clarity. It brings lighter energy that orients you correctly to improve your foundations. It delivers personal goals to the forefront of your life. Focusing on restoring stable foundations offers a pleasing result. Being willing to step back and contemplate the journey ahead restores and renews. A calming influence will help you maintain balance as you deal with hurdles and navigate life forward.

You can take your time to focus on building the foundations of your life. There is no hurry or need to rush this process. Incorporating healing into the basics of your life help nourish well-being and gently restores harmony. The wheels are in motion to bring new possibilities into your life. Healing the past has a therapeutic effect that draws more balance and well-being into your life. It unlocks a gateway towards an expressive and creative time of nurturing new areas. It helps you clear the decks for a fresh start as things begin to fall into place and life tempts you towards these new options. Sharing your thoughts and concerns with another draws a therapeutic aspect that offers to heal. You begin to take the first steps on a personal journey that holds meaning. It gives you the green light to connect with inspiration and pour your energy into a path that offers abundance. It does spotlight a supportive landscape that nurtures well-being ahead. It helps you plot a course you can grow.

Jupiter brings movement, change, action, and discovery into your life in conjunction with the Sun. A freedom-driven time offers a positive aspect that improves energy and enthusiasm for life. Being proactive encourages you to reach for your dreams. Forward momentum spurs you onward and helps you manifest goals. Inspiration and confidence rise, which boost heighten creativity, bringing significant results. Gathering your resources, you set off on a new journey forward for your working life. A highly productive chapter enables you to achieve your goals and advance your abilities forward. New energy arrives to shake up your life and bring new options to your table. Letting go of the past release blocks and enable you to move towards a new cycle in your working life.

New options arrive that promote success and abundance. You discover a new role for your career path that motivates and inspires you greatly. Full of energy and zeal for the prospects involved in this area, you be brimming with confidence as you feel success is looming. Optimism and good times run rife, creating a strong sense of well-being and happiness. Renewed optimism and positivity weave a basket of growth around your dreams and goals. Exploring new leads brings a path that offers growth and prosperity. Expanding horizons illuminate the way forward.

A New Moon in Taurus brings an option on offer at the week's end that grows your abilities and refines your talents. Concentrating on achieving your goals gives you clear insight into the path ahead. Your abilities are ready to shine; being open to new possibilities brings rewards and prosperity into your life. You find a new way of resolving issues that prevent progress. Adopting a unique perspective, getting fresh ideas and remarkable insight enables you to grow your life outwardly. As you place the final touches on your working goals, a window of opportunity opens, bringing new information into your life. It gives you an imprint that offers clues and insight into the path ahead

You are wise to stay open to fresh ideas and new possibilities for your life. The new year brings a clean slate of potential to your door. It offers an environment that nurtures freedom and expansion in your life. Listening to your inner wisdom draws a curious journey that moves you in alignment with growing your abilities. It marks a more prosperous life experience to light, one that sustains well-being and brings peace and happiness.

Nurturing your dreams influences your life, supporting well-being and grounded foundations. A lot of new energy is ready to emerge in your life. This week offers a productive chapter that helps you get the ball rolling on developing new goals for your life. It brings a bold chapter that lets you expand life outwardly and explore new horizons that nurture creativity and abundance.

Lyrids Meteor Shower illuminates an exciting landscape of potential this week. Opportunities to socialize bring excitement and news into your life. A prominent area sparks your interest and brings exciting potential into your situation. You are doing the right thing by exploring options on expanding life into a new journey forward. Opening a new page on your book of life revitalizes your spirit with refreshing possibilities. It opens the floodgates, which lights up inspiration.

The future looks rosy as you land in a new and exciting landscape soon. An avenue opens that draws lighter energy into your life. It brings a time of nurturing your home environment and improving the options in your world. It marks a slower pace that restores harmony and equilibrium. It helps you lay the groundwork to improve the foundations in your world. Focusing on the building blocks lets you make essential changes that progress life towards new possibilities and options. Your willingness to explore leads brings golden opportunities to light.

A shift forward draws a richly abundant path for your life. Enterprising options reveal an exciting landscape of possibility that helps connect you with inspiration. Investigating options brings a cycle of growth that offers expansion and learning. It brings a happy time of nurturing your creativity and growing your talents. A vibrant and exciting influence sparks a radiant frequency that revitalizes and restores your spirit.

MAY

Sun	Mon	Tue	Wed	Thu	Fri	Sat
	1	2	3	4	5	6
7	8	9	10	11	12	13
14	15	16	17	18	19	20
21	22	23	24	25	26	27
28	29	30	31			

May 1st - Mercury at Inferior Conjunction
May 1st Pluto retrograde begins in Aquarius

May 5th - Flower Moon. Full Moon in Scorpio 17:34
May 5th - Penumbral Lunar Eclipse

May 6th - Eta Aquarids Meteor Shower, April 19th - May 28th

May 9th - Uranus in Conjunction with Sun

May 12th - Last Quarter Moon in Aquarius 14:28

May 15th - Mercury Retrograde ends in Taurus

May 19th - New Moon in Taurus 15:54

May 27th - First Quarter Moon in Virgo 15:22

May 29th - Mercury at Greatest Elong: 24.9°W

NEW MOON

FULL MOON

Pluto's planet goes retrograde this week before a full Moon in Scorpio combines with a penumbral lunar eclipse. The Full Moon this week helps you cut away from outworn areas. Setting boundaries and moving away from toxic environments will hold you in good stead as it develops your world in the right direction. You can overcome barriers and move towards expansion. It brings a journey that offers completion and success. Bringing all parts seamlessly together enables you to achieve your goals.

Exploring leads get a newfound sense of direction as restraints lift, and you can move to the next level in your life. Possibilities ahead light a path forward towards a refreshing environment. You attract opportunities that hold promise, and being open to new options brings a gateway of growth into your life.

Opportunities to nurture your spirit provide an outlet that connects you with creativity and inspiration. It brings a fresh start that grows your abilities and nurtures your talents. A positive breakthrough or realization comes calling that lets you spot a journey worth developing. Mapping out goals supports expansion and places you in alignment to grow your world. An area you invest your time into developing draws a pleasing result. New options help cut away from areas best left behind. It places your focus forward in the most delightful way.

Uranus, in conjunction with the Sun, brings a curious surprise. Life gets a celebration that carries you along to a happier chapter. Exciting options ahead attract opportunities in several areas of your life. It charts a course towards increasing the stability and happiness in your world. News arrives that motivates you to craft plans and move forward towards launching an area of interest.

Being curious and exploring leads coaxes you to reach for your dreams. It brings a thoughtful influence that encourages you and lets you dare to dream and head towards your goals. Seeing potential projects and future options under the scope of your creativity brings newfound confidence. An emphasis on improving your life gets a bumper crop of potential to your door. You find effective ways to nurture your life and restore balance to your foundations. Indeed, you attract new possibilities into your life that lets you dip your toes in a sea of creativity.

You have gifts to share with a broader audience. You can trust your instincts to guide you to the right areas of learning as there is no right or wrong way to develop your abilities. Using creative or spiritual tools connects you with inspiration, increasing the flow of magic around your world. It lets you get busy designing your life and growing your situation into a new area.

Mercury retrograde ends in Taurus, which soon initiates growth in your social life draws pleasing changes that support well-being and nurture confidence. The conditions are ripening and sending you towards change. New options enhance your life and bring a burst of lightness and excitement as you get busy developing your dreams. It links you with kindred spirits who support your life by offering thoughtful discussions and sharing curious ideas and goals. A refreshing change flows into your life, imparts positivity, and draws blessings. It provides opportunities to mingle and network with lively friends and characters. A social aspect sets the tone for an abundant chapter that brings a boost into your life. Opportunities to expand your social circle abound; it introduces you to unique people and creative types.

You can enjoy a bright and happy time shared with friends. It dials down the stresses and restores equilibrium to your foundations. Many possibilities support growth and expansion in your life. Being open to growing your situation will form a stable foundation that nurtures your life in many ways. Decisions and choices ahead shape a journey of developing goals and dreams. Essential changes draw blessings as you get busy developing ideas and plans that nurture your life from the ground up. It brings a refreshing time that offers a sense of renewal and happiness. It attracts a buzz of activity that draws a social aspect that stabilizes foundations and brings lighter energy into your life.

Developing your unique skills and talents are links you up with positive change. Laying the groundwork for expansion one brick at a time fortifies foundations and gives you a strong basis from which to grow your world. You connect with inspiration, which gives you the green light to develop your abilities and heads towards growth and learning. Developments ahead bring news and potential flowing into your life. It brings the right environment to explore advancement. A new element enters your life soon. It brings opportunities that let you feel confident about developing new plans. As curious possibilities emerge, the tides turn in your favor. It charts a course towards change that moves you in alignment with exciting goals that light up creativity and inspiration. Having new possibilities to consider keeps motivation strong and helps you charge ahead towards growing your life. The right opportunity crops up that feel like the perfect fit for your life. It brings music into your world.

Increasing activity around your social life leads to developments and new potential. It attracts new friends, and this dynamic environment hits the ticket for a happy chapter of mingling and networking. You have a flair for bringing people together and sharing thoughts and ideas. Information arrives that launches a bold shift forward in your social environment. It draws a new friendship to light, which enriches and rewards. It underscores the energy of magic that surrounds your life at this time.

JUNE

Sun	Mon	Tue	Wed	Thu	Fri	Sat
				1	2	3
4	5	6	7	8	9	10
11	12	13	14	15	16	17
18	19	20	21	22	23	24
25	26	27	28	29	30	

ASTROLOGY

June 4th - Strawberry Full Moon: Sagittarius 03:42
June 4th - Venus at Greatest Elong: 45.4°E

June 10th - Last Quarter Moon in Pisces 19:31

June 17th - Saturn Retrograde begins in Pisces

June 18th - New Moon in Cancer 04:38

June 21st - Midsummer/Litha Solstice 14:52

June 26th - First Quarter Moon in Libra 07:50

June 30th - Neptune Retrograde begins in Pisces

FULL MOON

Venus reaches the greatest elongation as a full Moon in Sagittarius blooms. You settle into an avenue that offers abundance, creative expression, and happiness. Staying open to new pathways draws growth and attracts stellar opportunities into your life. Being proactive about expanding your life into a new area lets you move forward reasonably quickly towards unique horizons that call your name. It kicks off an exciting chapter where life enriches and offers a new and refreshing potential landscape.

Setting boundaries and distancing yourself from toxic environments is essential in nurturing happiness and harmony in your life. Life is ready to ripen with new potential on the way. It brings better opportunities to socialize with people who offer thoughtful dialogues and a genuine approach. Mingling with kindred spirits and friends sets the tone for a social phase that draws rejuvenating power into your surroundings.

You are ready to begin a new chapter. The power of intention plants the seeds that bring creativity into your world. It catalyzes change and instigates removing outworn areas from your life. You can trim the deadwood tree and grow fantastic new potential in your life. Exploring life with a unique perspective opens your world to refreshing possibilities. You benefit from events on the horizon as it lets you pass the threshold and enter a brighter chapter in your life.

Mercury lands in your fourth house of heritage, foundation, and home life. Mercury attracts stability and emphasizes study, learning, and education matters. Taking a slower approach can help nurture a balanced and secure basis that gives you a broader view of the path ahead.

Mercury in the fourth house teaches moderation, patience, perseverance, and balance. It is a stabilizing and harmonizing influence that restores well-being to your spirit. It may encourage you to make some changes in areas where you have been out of balance with your approach to life. Creating stable foundations enables you to move forward gently and adjust course as necessary. It centers your energy in a calming and soothing environment. It helps you take the middle road, creating sturdy foundations that keep life running smoothly.

Your willingness to explore new options for your life draws dividends. You hit a home run and begin developing your life outwardly. The conditions are perfect for extending your reach into a new area and taking an active role in developing your skills and refining your talents. Working with your abilities has a powerful effect as it provides you with a unique landscape of potential. Something on offer soon brightens your day.

The New Moon in Cancer before Midsummer/Litha Solstice at week's end brings refreshing vibrations into your life. Setting intentions lights a clear path forward that connects you with inspiration and creativity. A potent brew of manifestation is at your disposal. Exploring leads kicks off a chapter of growth and planning that sees developments occurring in your life that nurture your artistic side. A period of rapid growth brings expansion to your life. It gets a time of harmony and balance that offers peace and contentment. Good fortune shines as you cultivate happiness in your life. You move in a new direction that provides expansion and the development of a shared project. Building up the potential possible brings an enriching landscape into view.

Choices and decisions ahead drive expansion as an opportunity comes knocking. It brings empowering options that let you grow your world and head towards a brighter and happier chapter. It brings a windfall that moves you forward towards new possibilities. Nurturing your life encourages you to share your expertise with a broader audience. It brings a life-changing decision that grows your world and one that lets you reach for your dreams. Looking into your past and understanding the life lessons that have guided you to this juncture enable you to choose the correct path for your journey forward

The planet Neptune goes retrograde in Pisces. You move forward in life with an awareness of a deeper calling within your spirit. Life offers a balanced and purposeful path forward that lets you realign your goals with your changing emotional landscape. You get busy developing your life in alignment with the person you are becoming. Taking stock of your situation and planning the path enable you to express yourself through your studies and grow your world in a purposeful direction. Staying grounded, finding the middle ground for your life allow you to stay in the flow and recharge your batteries with inspiration and motivation. Staying true to your vision brings meaning and growth into your life. Serenity and peace provide a backdrop that sustains and nurtures well-being. There is no rush to reach the destination; a moderate and guided approach enables you to advance your career goals appropriately.

All the pieces of your puzzle finally come together to form a strategy that improves prospects for your career path. You become involved in nurturing an area opens up an approach that drives your passion and inspiration. It motivates you to follow your dreams towards advancing your skills and abilities into a new site. Moving in this direction brings new challenges and areas of learning and growth. Being objective and looking at all the possibilities ensures you grow your world in a happy and conscious approach.

Sun	Mon	Tue	Wed	Thu	Fri	Sat
						1
2	3	4	5	6	7	8
9	10	11	12	13	14	15
16	17	18	19	20	21	22
23	24	25	26	27	28	29
30	31					

July 1st - Mercury at Superior Conjunction

July 3rd - Buck Moon. Full Moon in Capricorn. Supermoon 11:40

July 10th - Last Quarter Moon in Aries 01:48

July 17th - New Moon in Cancer 18:32

July 23rd - Venus retrograde begins in Leo

July 25th - First Quarter Moon in Libra 22:06

July 28th - Delta Aquarids Meteor Shower. July 12th - August 23rd

NEW MOON

The Mercury at Superior conjunction. Full Moon in Capricorn, Supermoon. Healing can feel a little challenging as it brings new foundations on several levels. Closing the door on the past means you needn't carry the burden on your shoulders any longer. You may be feeling torn about heading in a new direction for your life. Still, this transition will nurture your spirit and rejuvenate your world from the ground up. Contemplating options brings insight into a remarkable journey forward.

A wave of opportunities breaks upon your shore and encourages you to head towards new horizons. News arrives that reminds you of a past chapter; it links you up with a sentimental theme that reverberates around your life during this time. A new option ahead anchors your energy in a project that offers a chance to launch your star to a lofty height. Self-expression and creativity are rising, boosting confidence and expanding your life outwardly. A river of awareness cultivates self-development and rules advancement in an area that inspires you on an emotional level.

Lively energy percolating in the background makes the dashing entrance into your world. It draws a bountiful time that nurtures entertaining discussions, insight, and news. Sharing with friends takes you towards a chapter that is brighter, lighter, and filled with good intentions. It encourages a strong foundation that restores balance.

Mercury heads to your sixth house and emphasizes routine tasks and duties. It brings rising attention to your career area and tasks performed in service to others in your life. Organization, efficiency, and productivity will be under the spotlight this week.

The care and attention to detail draw pleasing results that heighten security—your personal life benefits from your generosity in sharing all you have achieved. Job security and satisfaction are prominent as your dedication and discipline reward your life on many levels. You enjoy a secure and balanced foundation that offers a prosperous landscape in your life. It brings enriching moments that heighten well-being as it let you see a broad overview of your life in all you have achieved. It brings a time of celebration into your world that lets you taste the sweet flavor of success. It is a time that nurtures your spirit and draws well-being into your life.

Your career growth is moving into uncharted territory. You pursue developing your goals and dreams: overcoming obstacles and opposition drive self-improvement, confidence, and ability. Taking a stand for what you believe in helps you cross the threshold and advance towards a new level of growth in your life. It brings more balance into your surroundings, and you soon get settled in a productive and lively atmosphere. It generates plenty of leads that let you chart a path towards achievement and expansion.

This week a New Moon in Cancer brings a surge of confidence that helps you chart a course towards developing your life. This surprise news heightens creativity and offers the chance to learn the ropes of a new area. It puts you in the right direction to develop your skills and grow your talents. You have earned the right to nurture your life and make yourself a priority. You paint the backdrop to a blank canvas and create a masterpiece.

Being receptive to change and flexible brings a spontaneous and lively environment into view. You shift gears and embrace an influx of invitations and possibilities for your social life. You land in an entertaining and happy landscape filled with unique characters and thought-provoking discussions. Mingling with the crew of trailblazing characters brings fresh energy into your social life. It draws excitement and happiness.

As you expand your life outwardly, a new chapter of potential arrives to flip the switch on, lighting up a prosperous path forward. It raises confidence and brings developments that link to growing your personal life. It offers a heartwarming phase of strengthening bonds and sharing more in-depth communication. It lays the foundations for a stable and balanced journey that deepens a bond over time.

Venus retrograde begins in Leo, which slows potential around romance and personal bonds. Retreating and contemplating the path ahead help you connect with intuition and instinct to unearth your situation's secrets. It is a spiritually significant time that also offers healing through harmonizing frazzled nerves. It increases the introspective aspect and encourages you to engage in quiet contemplation. Deep thinking and inner searching light the path by providing innovative solutions. You may be about to face a decision in your life. Facing the truth of a situation shines a light on where the scales may be tipped unevenly to one side, creating a sense of imbalance in your life. As you move energy in alignment with the person you are ready to become, karmic forces guide and evolve your spirit. Being accountable for your actions enables you to step forward and achieve the highest result possible for your life.

Channeling the energy of compassion is a harmonizing aspect that enables you to draw balance into your life by creating space for peace and solitude. It draws insight and clarity into your world, allowing you to make adjustments and plan correctly.

You forge a stable path forward for your life. Sharing creative ideas with friends and loved ones brings new thoughts and ideas to explore. It takes you to a time of exploring innovative pathways and curious leads. Marching to the beat of your drum, you make the music that inspires your soul. It attracts an ex-self expressive and creative journey ahead.

AUGUST

Sun	Mon	Tue	Wed	Thu	Fri	Sat
		1	2	3	4	5
6	7	8	9	10	11	12
13	14	15	16	17	18	19
20	21	22	23	24	25	26
27	28	29	30	31		

August 1ˢᵗ - Full Sturgeon Moon in Aquarius Supermoon 18:32

August 8ᵗʰ - Last Quarter Moon in Taurus 10:28

August 10ᵗʰ - Mercury at Greatest Elong: 27.4°E

August 12ᵗʰ - Perseids Meteor Shower July 17ᵗʰ - Aug 24ᵗʰ

August 16ᵗʰ - New Moon in Leo 09:37

August 23ʳᵈ - Mercury Retrograde begins in Virgo

August 24ᵗʰ - First Quarter Moon in Sagittarius 09:57

August 27ᵗʰ - Saturn at Opposition

August 29ᵗʰ - Uranus Retrograde begins in Taurus

August 31ˢᵗ - Full Moon, Supermoon, Blue Moon in Pisces 01:36

NEW MOON

FULL MOON

Full Moon, Supermoon in Aquarius draws a healing and thoughtful vibe that surrounds your life. Your thoughts turn back to the past. Reconnecting with an emotionally rich journey helps nurture well-being. It brings a time of shedding the outworn energy and connecting with joy as you begin to wipe the slate clean and enter a fresh chapter. Strengthening your foundations brings a transformative time that offers to reshuffle the decks of potential in your life.

Unwrapping the chapter ahead brings a pleasant surprise that nurtures well-being. It helps push barriers back, as it marks a refreshing time that rules expansion in your social life. An attractive viewpoint comes into view and lands you in an exciting environment that offers a chance to mingle with friends. An emphasis on networking with your circle places you on the path towards developing interpersonal bonds.

An emphasis on your home life builds stable and secure foundations. It offers new possibilities that draw abundance into your home life. Adopting a gentle approach marks a pleasing result. You nurture an environment that provides a balanced path forward—opportunities to mingle, boost structure and stability and draw well-being into your world. Life becomes more settled as a nurturing influence flows into your world. Joy and warmth create a memorable centerpiece in your life that nurtures grounded foundations.

Perseids meteor shower ignites new possibilities. While things may feel up in the air, you soon land in a settled environment that connects you with friends and loved ones. A social aspect ahead brings refreshing potential into your world. An invitation to mingle nurtures well-being and offers thoughtful discussions with your broader circle of friends. Bright and cheerful energy flows into your life, harmonizing and balancing your spirit. It provides a chance to nurture grounded foundations and draw stability into your home life. It brings a radiant aspect that offers a lively and dynamic portal to a brighter chapter.

You can expand your horizons and enjoy exciting destinations. You enter an extended time that brings a boost into your world. It heals the old wounds that prevent progress and creates space for new possibilities to offer growth and expansion. Themes of abundance, security, and happiness secure a prosperous chapter. It provides a chapter that fosters creativity and nurtures new possibilities.

A unique chapter ahead offers rising prospects as life brims with refreshing options. Being open to developing new pathways brings growth and change into your life. It unleashes a positive trend that ushers in advancement around your career goals. You create a solid basis to shape the development of future dreams. A social aspect brings mingling with kindred spirits who offer thoughtful discussions.

The New Moon in Leo attracts potential. Change is around your situation as news lights up your life across the board with unique possibilities. Improvement may be rapid as you dive into a social aspect that offers growth. You have weathered a storm of choppy seas and now can embrace smooth sailing. It helps you reach a more prosperous foundation as improvement flows into your surroundings. It opens your life up to a new flavor.

Exciting mingling opportunities bring a gratifying theme that connects you with kindred spirits. It helps you forge several new possibilities for your social life as it brings unique friendships to light. It places your vision forward and is a time of growth and happiness. It shines a light on expanding your horizons and connecting with your circle of friends. The pace and rhythm of life pick up speed, bringing social activities that draw movement and discovery into your life. News arrives that gets a welcome boost.

Positive energy flows into your life, bringing a warm glow to your spirit. It sets the scene to nurture abundance as a positive influence arrives to boost well-being and harmony. You enter a richly enjoyable environment that promotes social ties and friendships. It brings the chance to mingle and share thoughtful discussions that enrich your world. Being open to new people and possibilities helps you rise above troubles and embrace an enriching social time.

Uranus retrograde begins in Taurus. Full Moon, Supermoon, Blue Moon in Pisces on the last day of the month. This Full Moon energy centers around stability and security. Pressure eases, reducing stress. It translates into a chapter where you can focus on projects and ventures that make the most of your creativity. Dabbling in your interests draws balance and abundance into your surroundings. It drives communication with friends that offer collaboration, growth, and kingship. It's a refreshing change as drama sweeps out to sea, and you can set sail on a new adventure that captures your interest.

A time of rejuvenation helps you move away from issues and release troublesome energy. As you shake off the heavy vibes that have clung to your power, you transition towards a happier chapter. You build foundations based on goals, dreams, and desires. Nurturing your creativity brings new pathways to explore. You create a shift forward that takes you towards a path of purpose and productivity.

A path of higher wisdom and learning comes calling. It illuminates change and brings options to develop a journey that speaks to your heart. It helps you navigate a complicated time and come out the other side more resilient. Life-affirming possibilities connect you with the tribe of kindred spirits, which lays the groundwork for a web of support.

SEPTEMBER

Sun	Mon	Tue	Wed	Thu	Fri	Sat
					1	2
3	4	5	6	7	8	9
10	11	12	13	14	15	16
17	18	19	20	21	22	23
24	25	26	27	28	29	30

September 4th - Venus Retrograde ends in Leo
September 4th - Jupiter Retrograde begins Taurus

September 6th - Last Quarter Moon in Gemini 22:21
September 6th - Mercury at Inferior Conjunction

September 15th - New Moon in Virgo 01:40
September 15th - Mercury Retrograde ends in Virgo

September 19th - Neptune at Opposition

September 22nd - Mercury at Greatest Elong 17.9°W
September 22nd - First Quarter Moon Sagittarius 19:32

September 23rd - Mabon/Fall Equinox. 06:50

September 29th - Corn Moon. Harvest Full Moon. Supermoon in Aries 09:58

NEW MOON

FULL MOON

This week, Venus retrograde ends. Jupiter retrograde begins in Taurus. Couples deepen a heart bond, and singles develop a potential love interest. Passion and fire energy ignite desire and love. Focusing time and energy on nurturing a romance in your life forge a deep connection between shared values and a unified approach. Unconditional love deepens a bond that grows into a deeply fulfilling journey forward for your romantic life.

Things are on the move for your social life soon. An exciting aspect flows into your world and lightens the atmosphere. You connect with those out of touch, which paves the way towards a more lively environment. Entertaining and connecting with your tribe is a theme that resonates with abundance. It gets the ball rolling on an enriching phase of expansion that sees a personal goal taking shape. Remember, when you lay your bets via your intuition, things soon fall into place, drawing a pleasing result.

Opportunities ahead improve the security in your life. Surprise developments draw refreshing possibilities into your life. It links up to a social and active environment that you share with friends and acquaintances. An area nurtured becomes a clear path forward. It brings a chapter that favors growth; it symbolizes rising prospects. It stirs inspiration and creativity, which cracks a brighter chapter ahead.

A time of restructuring ahead draws changes into your life. Moving away from areas that failed to reach fruition helps provide steady progress as you journey towards improving your circumstances. Indeed, information ahead that jumpstarts a new goal and leads to an exciting chapter of growing your life. Pushing past perceived limitations reveals an exciting landscape of growth is possible. It brings a creative landscape that nurtures new options. A winning possibility comes calling, which helps you boldly push the barriers back and head towards change.

Significant changes are heading your way. An invitation ahead hits a high note for your social life. It is a time that serves your spirit well as it draws rejuvenation and well-being into your life. It brings an enriching time shared with others, and this offers a welcome sense of connection in your world. An emphasis on improving your circumstances advances life forward towards new possibilities.

You soon hit your stride in a new chapter of growth, drawing stability into your life. It grounds your energy in an environment that offers a beautiful foundation from which to grow your world. A new goal comes to life that sparks lively discussions and trailblazing conversations. Skinny skies overhead restore your energy tanks, creating motivation and inspiration to grow your world. It brings a radiant aspect that draws blessings.

A New Moon in Virgo combines with Mercury retrograde ending this week. Life picks up steam, bringing new flavors and possibilities that inspire growth. Broadening horizons offers room to grow a path that sees potential blossoming. Being open to new leads encourages creative thinking. It lets you come up with a winning destination. It offers an enterprising approach that develops new goals.

A new chapter ahead draws beneficial and pleasing options into your world. It brings new beginnings that expand your life and grow your circumstances outwardly. It brings heightened motivation that has you feeling fired up about the journey ahead. Your pioneering approach blazes the way forward towards rising prospects.

You open the floodgates to a lucky chapter as the changes ahead clear the deck for the new potential to flourish in your world. An area you pour your energy into it is productive and rewarding. Setting your intentions creates potent alchemy that adds magic and inspiration to your ideas. Being proactive draws dividends as improvements swiftly follow the expansion of horizons. You ramp up opportunities by being open to change.

Mabon/Fall Equinox occurs this week with a Full Moon, Supermoon in Aries towards the week's end. You find new leads by broadening the perception of what is possible in your life. Limiting thoughts, beliefs, and outlooks prevent you from reaching your true potential. Exploring new possibilities for your life helps you establish a more empowered mindset that sees the glass as half complete. Releasing the deadwood and removing the thoughts and beliefs that hold you back improve your life. It connects with a supportive environment link you with others who support and nurture your life. It offers a chance to enhance the possibilities in your social life. Being proactive and focusing on self-development releases the chains that hold you back ushers in new options that expand your circle of friends.

Your efforts to improve your circumstances come up trumps when you discover a new role is on offer for your working life. You generate new leads for your career path that offers financial security, which gives you the ability to build stable foundations in your life. Rising career prospects grow your life in a successful direction. As you head towards growth and prosperity, you invest wisely and secure a more solid foundation in your life. Being resourceful, practical, and hard-working brings a balanced and stable journey forward for your working life. Creating an established routine and being diligent advance your career ahead. You discover a lead that offers tangible results; it brings the right time to reinvent yourself in a new professional situation.

Sun	Mon	Tue	Wed	Thu	Fri	Sat
1	2	3	4	5	6	7
8	9	10	11	12	13	14
15	16	17	18	19	20	21
22	23	24	25	26	27	28
29	30	31				

October 6th - Last Quarter Moon in Cancer 13.48

October 7th - Draconids Meteor Shower. Oct 6th -10th

October 11th - Pluto Retrograde ends in Capricorn

October 14th - New Moon in Libra 17:54
October 14th - Annular Solar Eclipse 17:59

October 20th - Mercury at Superior Conjunction

October 21st -Orionids Meteor Shower. Oct 2nd – Nov 7th

October 22nd - First Quarter Moon Aquarius 03.29

October 23rd - Venus at Greatest Elong: 46.4°W

October 28th - Partial Lunar Eclipse 20:14
October 28th - Hunters Full Moon in Taurus 20:23

NEW MOON

This week, Mercury settles into your eighth house of finances, resources, and rebirth. Information arrives that brings an entrepreneurial direction. It lets you advance your interests into a new area. Focusing on preparing the path ahead draws progression. You enter a highly productive time that is ripe for expansion. You benefit from events on the horizon as they let you gather your resources while planning the strategy for growth in finances.

You may feel unsettled, directing your attention to exploring new growth pathways. There may be a goal in the long range, but it soon comes into view as an area worth pursuing. Channeling your energy into planning the course draws dividends. It lets things fall into place, providing you with the stepping stones forward. A dream may suddenly be within reach. A potent influence of growth tempts you towards your vision.

Extra opportunities are opening soon that open the gates to a busy time. It brings an initiative that offers advancement. An organized approach provides a winning strategy. A new role makes an entrance, and it gets a lead ripe for growth. Staying open to new possibilities, people, and resources, feed your creativity with new potential. Exciting changes are coming up that draw abundance.

Pluto retrograde ends in Capricorn. New Moon in Libra at the week's end combines with an annular solar eclipse. A new beginning ahead for your career path. It brings a fresh start on many levels as it does entail learning and growing your skills. It cracks the code to a brighter chapter. It offers security, growth, and progression. A new role is on offer that takes your skills towards advancement.

News arrives that earmarks a new beginning for your life. It brings an active and progressive chapter that offers a shift forward towards developing new goals. It brings a window of opportunity that helps get life back on track with endeavors that capture your interest. Opening the gates wide to these possibilities shines a light on a happy and abundant landscape. Being open to change facilitates growth; it allows you to grow your abilities and work with your talents. An area you become involved with takes shape and gets excellent satisfaction in your world.

You are ready to usher in a new journey. It takes your skills to new heights. There is a strong focus ahead on what is truly important to you. It does bring time to work through issues that hold your potential back. Planning the course lets you develop innovative solutions that clear the decks for a fresh start. You approach life with a unique flair that amplifies your success rate.

Mercury at Superior conjunction brings a time that nurtures creativity and illuminates new possibilities. As your landscape broadens, you attract new options into your world, which grows your circle of friends. It brings a time of active and insightful discussions that set the scene for future growth. A busy time opens the way forward as you can embrace entertaining and sharing with friends and loved ones.

Improving your social life brings inner happiness, contentment, satisfaction, and joy. Your heart overflows with abundance when you forge a new friendship that aligns with your hopes and dreams. Indulging in life's pleasures brings an abundant landscape that lets you enjoy all that life has to offer. It has you feeling grateful for an emerging connection that becomes closer as you open your life up to another person. An open vessel points you towards a path of growing dreams and nurturing dreams. A relationship you invest your time into be a joyful and positive bond in your life. Improvement ahead in your circumstances is a happy time that helps you grow your life. Your dreams and wishes are coming into reality as you see tangible progress occurring in your life.

An invitation ahead hits a highlight for your social life. A whirlwind of activity brings excitement into your life. It charts a course towards an enriching chapter that draws stability and improves the building blocks of foundations.

This week, a partial lunar eclipse blends magic with a Full Moon in Taurus. It speaks of the transition ahead that involves soul-searching. Taking time to pull back and contemplate your future life direction draws an exciting chapter of growing your world. It links you up with a pathway that offers room to develop your talents and nurture your abilities. Refining your inherent gifts lets you explore a side journey that feels right for your soul. It enables you to invest your time wisely in an area that is a soothing balm for your restless spirit.

The adventure of a lifetime ushers into your life soon. It opens a window of opportunity that gets a life on track to expand outwardly. It brings options that give you a brighter picture of what is possible in your world when you explore new possibilities. Information arrives that broadens the scope of potential around your life. It takes your talents further, enabling you to advance your abilities into a new area. It offers an assignment that inspires growth and learning. It brings a chance to work alongside others who share similar skills.

Small changes can create extensive pathways towards growth. Look for signs and serendipity that help your dreams take flight. Developing your vision draws momentum and progress into your life. Your goals take shape, and you soon discover an open road of exciting options that tempt you forward. It marks the type of journey that redefines what is possible in your world when you allow your creativity to bloom.

NOVEMBER

Sun	Mon	Tue	Wed	Thu	Fri	Sat
			1	2	3	4
5	6	7	8	9	10	11
12	13	14	15	16	17	18
19	20	21	22	23	24	25
26	27	28	29	30		

November 3rd - Jupiter at Opposition

November 4th - Saturn Retrograde ends in Pisces

November 4th - Taurids Meteor Shower.Sept 7th - Dec 10th

November 5th - Last Quarter Moon in Leo 08:37

November 13th - Uranus at Opposition
November 13th - New Moon in Scorpio 09:27

November 17th - Leonids Meteor Shower Nov 6th -30th

November 18th - Mars in Conjunction with Sun

November 20th - First Quarter Moon in Aquarius 10.50

November 27th – Beaver Moon. Full Moon in Gemini 09:16

NEW MOON

FULL MOON

Jupiter at opposition. Saturn retrograde ends in Pisces. Saturn moving into a direct phase emphasizes creating structure and progress in your life. Exploring diverse options supports a journey of growth and evolution. It lets you land in a productive atmosphere that is ripe with potential. Opportunities to mingle set the scene to expand your social life with new friends and companions. It brings a happy chapter that rules a time of expansion and harmony. It brings thoughtful discussions that offer cutting-edge ideas, which blaze a trail towards a path of inspiration.

Things head to an upswing soon. Life offers new possibilities that draw stability and balance into your world. It helps you navigate forward towards greener pastures. Making yourself a priority brings a turning point as it connects you to people who support your growth and evolution. It opens the door to revolution and renewal. The strength in your spirit offers the ability to push back barriers and create a bridge towards a brighter chapter.

Being open to change places you in the proper alignment to progress your circumstances towards developing a new area. You make a decision that cracks the code to a brighter chapter. It emphasizes self-development and working with your skills and abilities to advance life forward towards greener pastures. It is a journey that aligns with the person you are becoming. News arrives that points you in the right direction.

The planet Uranus is in opposition as the New Moon occurs in Scorpio. This week will be a fun chapter that delivers warmth, friendship, and advancement. Doors open and head you towards a social environment that stimulates creativity and energizes your spirit. Friends prominently figure in your life as expansion hits your social life. You meet new people and engage with expanding horizons under a social sky. It will bring an opportunity to widen your circle of friends and contacts.

A sense of celebration and camaraderie fills the air as you embrace a social aspect that feels emotionally rich and satisfying. Surrounded by friends, you enjoy a busy time building a rapport with people who offer thoughtful dialogues and stimulating discussions. Nurturing bonds will let you catch up with old friends, and this brings feelings of comfort and encouragement to your spirit.

As your social life expands, it creates space for new adventures to take flight. It draws abundance and invites joy into your world. New possibilities ignite your interest and make a shift forward that becomes a significant turning point for your life. Social invitations tempt you out in your broader community. This expansion kicks off a pivotal time where you connect with unique people and possibilities.

Leonids Meteor Shower lights up incredible energy this week. In conjunction with the Sun, Mars illuminates temptations, desires, and chemistry. It signifies new possibilities flowing into your social life. Invitations light up across the board and bring an influx of options into your world. You activate rising confidence, magnetism, and allure. It amplifies potential and brings a social aspect that lets you achieve growth in heart matters— romance, magic, and companionship light a trailblazing path forward.

It shows a busy time ahead that focuses on building interpersonal bonds. A potent mix of manifestation, inspiration, and transformation guides the path forward. Like-minded people are attracted to your energy, happiness, and harmony carry you along towards expanding your circle of friends. It brings an active environment that connects you with people who share compatible interests and values.

Life brings new energy into your personal life that inspires and delights. It lets you discover a situation that holds promise. You draw a journey that brings abundance, happiness, and progression. Sharing time with someone holds the key to growth. It puts you on the path to a connected and thriving future. It brings a lively time that nurtures your social life and brings a deepening of connection into your world. It lights a path of romance and magic that feels right for your life.

The Full Moon in Gemini helps release the heavy vibes and outworn energy clinging to your spirit. Life has been challenging, but a new beginning is looming overhead that breathes fresh air into your environment. It brings nourishment for your soul and sees your efforts to improve your life draw a pleasing result. It helps you focus on an area that offers room to improve your circumstances.

A crossroads ahead brings two choices into your life. Information forward encourages you to walk a path in alignment with the person you are becoming. Transforming the potential flowing into your life builds better foundations that offer room to grow into a journey of wisdom and growth. It draws an environment that is soul-affirming and enriching. Lighter energy flows into your life with a gust of fresh air.

Healing the past facilitates a new chapter. It brings some restructuring and sensitive areas that can trigger issues. However, reframing goals, broadening your perception enables personal growth to take the lead. Nurturing your life and making yourself a priority feeds creativity and heightens the potential possible in your world. It brings a more prosperous life experience that reawakens a sense of adventure. News is coming that guides the path forward. It brings clarity as a puzzle piece reveals; you discover the way ahead clears. It helps you turn a corner and enjoy smooth sailing.

DECEMBER

Sun	Mon	Tue	Wed	Thu	Fri	Sat
					1	2
3	4	5	6	7	8	9
10	11	12	13	14	15	16
17	18	19	20	21	22	23
24	25	26	27	28	29	30
31						

December 4th - Mercury at Greatest Elong: 21.3°E

December 5th - Last Quarter Moon in Virgo 05:49

December 6th - Neptune Retrograde ends in Pisces

December 12th - New Moon in Sagittarius 23:32

December 13th - Geminids Meteor Shower. Dec 7th - 17th
December 13th - Mercury Retrograde begins in Capricorn

December 19th - First Quarter Moon Pisces 18:39

December 21st - Ursids Meteor Shower Dec 17th -25th

December 22nd - Yule/Winter Solstice at 03:28
December 22nd - Mercury at Inferior Conjunction

December 27th - Cold Moon. Moon Before Yule. Full Moon in Cancer 00:34

December 31st - Jupiter Retrograde ends in Taurus

NEW MOON

FULL MOON

Neptune retrograde ends in Pisces. It connects you with kindred spirits who offer a fresh perspective and lively discussions. You seek spiritual wisdom and knowledge that establishes a set of values and beliefs that feel right for your life. Listening to teachers or mentors brings new insight that revolutionizes the potential possible in your world. Following your truth bring goodness into your life.

The openness that flows from your heart boosts your creativity and light up abilities to grow your talents. Letting your imagination and intuition unfurl new possibilities in your life bring a great deal of radiance and happiness into your world. You seek out advice and gather support from friends and loved ones before embarking on growing the path ahead.

A social aspect ahead sweeps away negativity and releases outworn energy. It brings a positive influence that offers a brighter, more optimistic vibe for your life. Focusing on improving your circumstances brings a gentle flow of abundance into your world. It brings a curious chapter that lets you nurture a new friendship. Sharing thoughtful and entertaining discussions is a welcome remedy that focuses on uplifting your spirit. It brings a turning point that adds the right flavor to your social life. Changes ahead nourish your environment and provide you with the right ingredients to add spice to your life.

The New Moon is in Sagittarius this week, with Mercury going retrograde the day afterward. You need a new approach as the Mercury retrograde disruption causes upheaval to your best-laid plans. A downturn in forwarding momentum brings disruption and change to your environment. It brings a spiritual aspect that encourages you to dig deeper and reveal insight and clarity into your larger goals. As you tune in to your life purpose, you discover a journey that holds excellent meaning is possible for your life. Research, planning, and cultivating your dreams enable you to grow your life in a prosperous manner. It brings a thought-provoking path that highlights possibilities that grow your world.

A sentimental theme brings your thoughts back to the past. A time of healing, reflection, and contemplation help release sadness and melancholy. As one year comes to a close, your thoughts traverse back and gain a deeper understanding of a situation you are leaving behind in your life. Creating space to honor your emotions and think about life on a deeper level provide you with insight and clarity. A time of introspection brings evaluation into your personal life. Disengaging from activities brings a thought-provoking chapter of soul-searching and healing into your life. It helps close the door to the past and mentally and emotionally prepare you for your next journey. It clears the slate for a fresh chapter of potential to enter your life early next year.

Ursids Meteor Shower lights up the sky with potential. An emphasis on your social life draws a pleasing result that lets you create tracks towards mingling and networking with friends. It marks a journey that offers enriching experiences and enchanting moments. You reveal new possibilities around your social life that opens the door to a fresh start. Spontaneous get-togethers and curious news lift the lid on a chapter of growth.

Information arrives that connects you with a social event. An invitation lights up your life. It points the way to a happy chapter of networking with friends and sharing thoughtful ideas and dialogues. It draws stability and grounds your energy in a heartwarming landscape. There is a lot of unique potential around your life that opens a path of increasing creativity that nurtures new possibilities in your life.

Events ahead attract exciting opportunities into your life. New options come knocking to face your attention towards growing your life in a unique direction. It marks a significant time that becomes a gateway to expand your world. Endless possibilities fascinate and mesmerize as you contemplate the path ahead with an eye for detail. It is sweeping away areas that failed to reach fruition that kicks off a journey that inspires growth. It touches you down in a landscape that offers a breakthrough. Life is ready to transform your world for the better.

Yule/Winter Solstice at the beginning of the week with a Full Moon in Cancer midweek, followed by Jupiter retrograde ending on the last day of the year in Taurus. Life brings a karmic ending into your life. As one door closes, it feels fair and reasonable to move in alignment with your higher self. Being ethical and righteous hold you in good stead. Being responsible for your actions and accountable for your choices and decisions helps you rise above drama and conflict in your social life.

Opportunities ahead link up a more social environment for your life. Offering impartial guidance and not swaying from your views show others you are a solid and capable person. You provide advice and wise counsel to someone who seeks you out and leans on you for support.

Thoughtful discussions ahead bring news and information into your life. Listening to your intuition lets, you trust your instincts and share correct information with someone who needs your help. Your thoughtful words and helpful advice bring positive outcomes into your world. It brings a new beginning into your life that lights up pathways of creativity and growth. You move in alignment with your intuition and harness the raw emotions within your spirit to create an abundant path towards a brighter future. You share good times and thoughtful discussions with someone who holds significant meaning in your life. The love you share with another person in your life return, making a happy and nurturing life. You see unique potential in the options surrounding your life.

NOTES

Dear Stargazer,

I hope you have enjoyed planning your year with the stars utilizing Astrology and Zodiac influences. My yearly zodiac books feature horoscopes weekly (four weeks to a month).

https://mystic-cat.com/

Instagram: SiaSands

Leaving a review is welcomed and appreciated.

Bright Blessings,

Sia Sands

Printed in Great Britain
by Amazon

12374150R00071